How to Get Your Shine On: From the Inside Out

Ivan Campuzano

SPECIAL THANKS

To my family, you mean everything to me.
I would like to thank my good friend and C.E.O coach Debra Benton who was the first to encourage me to put my ideas down on paper. Thank you for your advice and insight, it has been invaluable.

CONTENTS

My goal is show you how great you already are and essentially take you from where you are to where you want to be—by developing your inner being and leveraging technology to reach your dreams.

If you would like to contact me, write me at:
ivan@ivancampuzano.com

You can also follow me on Twitter: http://twitter.com/ivancampuzano

As one of my favorite rap artists Notorious B.I.G says:
"Stay far from timid,
only make moves when your heart is in it,
and live the phrase, sky's the limit"

INTRODUCTION

I have begun to live my life based on the questions I have asked myself and the research I have done regarding those questions (seek and you shall find). The only thing that makes us truly human is that we possess the power of choice—every day we have the power to decide anything for ourselves.

You will know when you are on the right path because you will feel great about what you are doing. People say there is great virtue in struggling for goals, and I agree partially with that idea. The wisdom lies in that as soon as you realize that the situation is not serving your higher purpose, the situation has served its purpose and it's time to move on. The problem for most people is that it takes time to change, but a true change is instant.

This is why it's important to do everything in your power to change your attitude and actions, after you identify that you are in a place that no longer serves you in order to move to a better place. All personal growth comes from a place of understanding yourself. You will soon begin to look at challenges in a different way—see them as they truly are, an opportunity to overcome the obstacle and be one step closer to your desire.

All you think you are is the amalgamation of the sum total memories of your entire life and yourself. The longer you are in a place you don't want to be, the more effort it takes to get on the right track. We are creatures of habit. As we become identified to our habits, we create a false identity around who we think we are. They may help you find your place in society, but if you don't put your future in your hands, you will identify yourself with your circumstances which for many of us will be negative in nature— I'm a failure, I'm not good enough. Now you have put your future in jeopardy because you are letting external circumstances control you.

Never give power to anything outside of yourself; otherwise, you are a puppet on strings. Remember, you have no control over anything outside of yourself. You must develop discipline and accept 100% responsibility for your life. True discipline is the most important, because once you become disciplined, you have achieved inner harmony and mastered your inner self.

When I say accepting 100% responsibility, I mean every facet of life-- everything is a reflection of your inner self—the job you chose, the friends you have, your environment, things you do, hobbies, interests, etc. You possess the power to choose; at one point you consciously or subconsciously chose everything you experienced in your life. Obviously, bad things can happen to good people, but it's important we don't identify with our temporary circumstances in order to minimize the time it takes to move forward. Otherwise, we may be end up creating a hole and then trying to dig ourselves out. Learning to live our life more mindfully our judgment will grow with experience. Learn not to judge your situations but learn to judge your actions. As you learn to tap into your inner stillness you will learn to hear the nudges from your real conscience that can distinguish what is right or wrong for you. Are your actions in line with your true desires and higher purpose?

"All perfection and every divine virtue are hidden within you. Reveal them to the world" - Babaji

You are already great and everything you need is already inside of you; my goal is to help you realize this and jumpstart your journey. You really can get to where you want to be and enjoy the life you are meant to have. Many of us grew up with the perspective that we need to become good at school, work, sports, etc.; always thinking we are not good enough until we have accomplished those things. This game called life is about realizing who you already are, and you are an amazing, unique human being.

In our culture, we have been conditioned for individual differences to stand out; we look to people and classify them as smart, dumb, rich, poor, ugly, or good looking. You feel powerless because you're always competing; you should only compete with yourself. Embrace yourself and continually develop your talents and inner being. If you solely focus on self-realization, you will see that humans are just part of one huge conscious organism, and we are more alike than different—we all essentially want the same things. No one sees the world through your eyes, and no one can offer the same perspective as you. Learn to not overestimate other people and never underestimate yourself.

"Benchmarking against the universe actually encourages us to be mediocre, to be average, to just do what everyone else is doing... Instead of benchmarking everything, perhaps we win when we accept that the best we can do is the best we can do, and then try and find the guts to do one thing that's remarkable" - Seth Godin

Ivan's Blueprint for Achieving Anything:

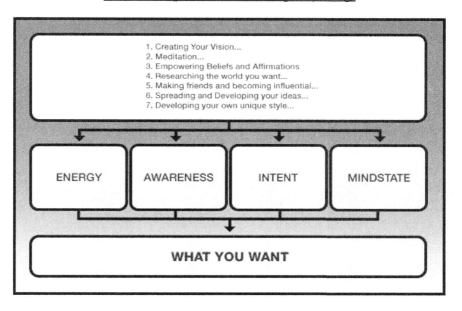

This book contains concepts that I feel you should continually refine, because they will all build on each other to help you reach personal fulfillment. You will experience what athletes call being "in the zone"—when your inner being, energy, awareness, intent, and mind state, are working congruently in the present.

"Success is the progressive realization of a worthy ideal"

Don't put so much pressure on yourself; know that personal evolution is a process and it's going to happen in its own special way. Learn to enjoy life as you go, and one day, you will wake up and realize you have and became everything you wanted.

Your journey towards your dreams will be a process, and most of that process is exploring your worst enemy. Many of you might realize that your mind has limited you more than it's helped. Don't hate yourself for this; realize that the mind is great at protecting you from what it doesn't understand. With greater understanding and a clear vision our egoic minds

3

can also turn into our biggest ally.

Your dreams are in the realm of the unknown and haven't materialized yet, and your mind has been conditioned to be skeptical of things that it can't see. Your ego is that little voice that you hear, or feel inside yourself, whenever you experience something. If you're shopping and see something you want, what immediate things do you feel and think? Deep down you know that having that outfit will make you feel great. What does the little voice say? If it says that it would be nice, but that you don't have enough money, or that people will judge you for wearing it—that's your ego trying to protect you from your dreams.

Your dreams might just be an idea, or visualization, in your head, and your ego becomes afraid of the uncertainty of that even becoming a reality. It makes up clever excuses to keep you safe. Instead of buying the flashier outfit that would make you feel good, you take home the safer look that will be accepted by others, because you might not have the confidence to wear the desired outfit.

Dreams require faith and confidence to take action into the unknown. The unknown is uncomfortable at first, but this is where you make dreams come true. Let go of any mental pictures holding you back. It might feel like you're losing your identity as you let go of these old images and beliefs that define you. You may have to lose yourself in order find yourself. Just remember that you can only lose what's false, what's true and intrinsic to your nature can never be lost. When we know everything that we are not, we discover who we truly are and has been there all along.

Your ego thinks in terms of identifying with the past and anticipating the future, depriving you of fully experiencing the present. This is where many people relate to the experience of being, "lost in thought," because your mind is consumed in trying to process too many inconsistent thoughts, mostly dealing with your past and future. When you have mastered your ego and inner self, you will truly live and experience the present moment. Once your mind is free of the internal chatter you will be in a better position to deliberately control your energy, awareness, intent, and mind state. The mind is a beautiful servant but a terrible master. This is when you will experience the sought after state of mind we call, "peace of mind."

My Definition of:

1. Energy- When I talk about energy, it is physical, mental, or spiritual. That's why being healthy is very important, if you don't have the physical energy the actions you take towards your goals will not be sufficient to see results. Mental energy is also very important, because even if you have all the physical energy in the world, but lack the mental energy and clarity, your energy won't be used on productive actions. If you are lacking a healthy spiritual energy, what you are pursuing might not have enough personal meaning and fulfillment.

2. Awareness- This means having the mental clarity to objectively see and feel yourself in the present moment. I like to think of it like Spider Man's ability to sense danger. Your awareness will enable you to see and sense things that most people can't see, because of their mental conditioning.

You will also develop and learn to trust your gut feeling. This awareness comes from developing your inner self and inner processes. The more acquainted you become with how you work internally, the better decisions you will make, because you will understand the reasons behind your actions.

3. Intent- This is your will or purpose for a specific outcome, which can be in your conscious or subconscious awareness.

4. Mind State- These are thought patterns that run all day in your mind. You have many different mind states that will produce certain results. Every day you are bombarded with visual stimulation from your environment. How you filter all the immense information and interpret it depends on your mindset.

Learn to control and use your energy wisely. Our negative emotions are one of the biggest factors that drain our energy and prevent our inner transformation. Learn to not express or repress your negative emotions. We must bring enough awareness to just release our tight grip around them. You need to have enough energy and awareness of the present moment, so when the right person, thing or idea shows up, you can recognize it and take immediate action. When you truly live with energy, awareness, intent, and proper mindset, you will see that things like coincidences are not really coincidences.

They are situations that you have asked for or thought about on some level (consciously or unconsciously), but because of a lack of awareness, you see them as a random event. Increasing your awareness will transform things like coincidences into moments of incredible insight that can lead to a personal epiphany. You see how each phase in your life has played out, the power of your decisions, and the direct impact they had on your life.

The first few months that I moved to Prague, I had the freedom to use my time on whatever I wanted. There were days when I did nothing; society has made us believe that doing nothing is unproductive and that you should always be on the move. I found that in the stillness of just being, great insights to questions would come to me. The only way to create this sense of knowingness is through an actual experience. Someone who takes life head on in the moment will enjoy the benefits of a rapid learning curve, and absorb the nuances to something much quicker.

Create a timeline of your entire life

Write down every moment and event (good or bad; it's important to be completely honest with yourself) that defined and shaped you. Write down as much as you can: what you were thinking, how you felt, and your beliefs at the time.

Study it and see how the decisions you made impacted your future. When we look to our past, we remember it only how we want to. Often, what really happened is not how we remember it. We must learn to see ourselves more objectively. An attachment to a past that didn't happen is very limiting because it's affecting your present decisions.

Train yourself to have an open mind; this will help you to see something that you might not be aware of, because your level of understanding can't see past it. Once I began to take an objective snapshot of my life, and incorporate everything I learned, my life began to feel like a jigsaw puzzle with more and more pieces coming together effortlessly. I used my past in a very productive way to create my future.

A lot of us go through life with the hope that things just fall into place. It's like you're trying to put together the jigsaw puzzle with your eyes closed, this will take more pain and energy. My intention is to give you the inner confidence and awareness to piece together the jigsaw puzzle with eyes wide open. When you reach these moments of mental clarity every idea you have feels right, things go your way, you overcome obstacles, and you find out what you're good at and what your purpose is in life.

Some things I identified that I wanted in my near future:

1. I wanted a job that allowed me the freedom to live and do whatever I

wanted.

2. Time to find my purpose and what I wanted to work on for the next few years.

3. A beautiful girlfriend inside and out.

4. Help people, because ultimately contributing to the greater good of everyone is the highest form of personal fulfillment that you can experience.

5. I love to travel and wanted to be in an environment where I am constantly stimulated.

When I identified everything that I wanted, and put all my energy and focus into it, magical things began to happen. In less than one year from college graduation, I quit my job and moved to one of the most beautiful cities in the world, Prague, Czech Republic. I had the freedom to work for myself and choose what I wanted to do every day. I traveled regularly to different countries. I dated extremely beautiful, intelligent, and cultured girls.

Most important, I found my purpose in life and have begun to work solely on achieving every experience that will add to my ultimate experience. I have the confidence in knowing nothing is out of my reach. I proved to myself the power that I possess.

Faith

All faith is, is having the power (trust in yourself) and energy to take the first step towards your goals and dreams. If you haven't taken the first step towards your dreams, you are lacking faith and a desire to have the things that will make you happy. You probably don't know what you really want from life. You might also feel that you're not worthy or it's selfish to have great things in your life. There is nothing wrong in going after things that will enable you to express your inner happiness. Our Beingness is happiness itself, so have the courage to discover who you really are by taking the leap in the unknown.

1 CREATING YOUR VISION

"Without a vision, the people will perish" – Solomon, Proverbs 28:19

One of the most important ingredients for success is having a clearly defined and vivid vision of where you want to be. At first the "how" is not that important, you need to create a vision that gets you so excited that you develop the attitude that you will stop at nothing to get what you want. Many people first focus on the how, and then quickly find themselves overwhelmed with too many details before talking themselves out of pursuing their goals.

You have to take a leap of faith and trust that the how will be shown to you as you go along. Do you remember the days as a child with dreams of unlimited possibilities? What happened to those dreams? You got older and domesticated by a society that says those dreams are foolish. Why wouldn't you want to accomplish the things that as a child you knew would make you happy? I encourage you to dream like you once used to.

"Shoot for the moon...even if you miss, you'll still be amongst the stars"

One way I keep myself motivated and my vision alive is through my picture book. Every morning, I look at it to remind me what I want in life. Go right now and get some magazines, cut out every picture of the things you want and places you want to visit—dare to dream. Look at your picture book until it becomes as vivid as possible in your mind. Taste the pina colada, feel the ocean breeze. Use anything you can to motivate you to achieve those feelings. The better you get at remembering times that truly made you happy—visualizing the way you want things to be—they may eventually manifest in your physical reality. How you feel is of ultimate importance; it is one of the main ways you attract anything in your life. You don't attract what you want, you attract what you are. What must the qualities of your inner Being be in order to reflect the things you truly desire? Learn to objectively see your daily attitudes in your day-to-day life to check if you're on the right track.

Tip: Before starting your day, meditate on the feeling of when you have amazing confidence. Think about how you think, act, and dress when you have this confident feeling. See yourself at the Starbucks acting confident. Now go to Starbucks and train yourself to maintain this attitude and mentality. See how this affects your experience at Starbucks.

"Reality is merely an illusion, albeit a very persistent one" – Albert Einstein

Making Your Vision a Reality

1. Decide what you're committed to achieving

2. Take immediate and massive action (research)

3. Test and refine your strategies

4. Change your approach until you get what you want

Exercise: To get a better sense of the vision you want to create; you need to explore your true desires. Take out a piece of paper and answer these questions:

--What material things do I want?

--What experiences do I want that fully engage my senses?

--What kind of relationships do I want?

--How can I contribute for the good of all?

When your answers become a part of a congruent vision, the doubt will not be the challenge that it might seem now.

Here are some points to consider when envisioning the person, you want to become, and the business or idea that you want to pursue. If you can answer these questions, I believe that you will stay ahead of the curve and give yourself better chances to succeed in our highly competitive, global world.

1. Can someone overseas accomplish the dream cheaper? If so, will you be able to stay profitable? What kind of business model and relationships will you need to develop?

2. Can a computer do it faster? Can technology replace your job or future career? Can you change your roll without becoming irrelevant or changing industry?

3. Am I offering something that satisfies immaterial desires?

The western society has become so efficient at making things that it has an abundance of material wealth. Many people find that the things they thought would make them happy is not satisfying or fulfilling. While material things are pleasing, we are ultimately after non-material spiritual meaning. When brainstorming ideas, consider if it will satisfy intangible desires. This ensures that your contribution is meaningful and will positively affect others' lives.

"As the choices available to business and consumers become increasingly clear and easily comparable, you've got to either be different or cheaper. You will fail if you try and do both – or neither."
- Seth Godin

"If you cannot find meaning in your life, it is your responsibility as a human being to create it, whether that is fulfilling your dreams or finding work that gives you purpose and self-worth- ideally a combination of both" - Tim Ferris

There is no doubt that when you contemplate some of these personal topics, you will have doubts. Just remember that doubts are no more than a signal that you must take action; many doubts are based on nonsense or from a lack of true information.

You must begin to quit consulting with the group mentality. Letting yourself be guided by the outside world is giving yourself permission to slowly evolve. If your inner voice tells you to do something, take Nike's advice and just do it, if you wait for everyone else, you might never start. Once you form a habit of not consulting with the group conscious mentality, you will let your individuality shine through and be closer to who you really are. The real you can be felt and seen when you are demonstrating and living the qualities of intelligence, alertness, wisdom, knowingness, and being tuned into your environment.

Become familiar with the different aspects of your identity to decide if they are congruent with the future vision of yourself:

1. Self-Image ("I think"): Examine the way you think, and you will see if it's conducive with who you want to become. If your current thoughts run contrary to that vision, it is a self-sabotage.

2. Self-Esteem ("I feel"): To have a positive and healthy self-esteem, change your self-image. If you feel a strong emotional discomfort in life, you have locked yourself into a false identification.

3. Self-Confidence ("I act"): As soon as your thoughts and feelings are in accord, the actions you take will come from a place that feels right to you, and the by product will be increased confidence in yourself and what you are doing.

The ego (false sense of self) promotes confusion because it wants to prove your separateness from everyone and everything. You have been conditioned to derive your sense of self and identity from your thoughts. Many people live their lives thinking they are their thoughts and mind. Thinking without awareness binds you to deeply engrained thought patterns. When you become aware that you are thinking that awareness is not part of thinking. You will realize that your true identity is pure consciousness, and not the thoughts and ideas your consciousness had identified with. Believing that you are your ego and thoughts will push you in the direction of judgment, comparison, and insist on being right and superior to others. Don't get caught up; begin by listening to the voice— your highest self—that wants you to be at peace. Deep down you know what things will bring you peace or take you further away from that state of being.

"In whatever situation you find yourself, always do your best, and let

all your decisions and path of action come from your heart." - Babaji

Practice the attitude of appreciating your current situation, while being clear of where you want to be, and the steps needed to get there. Whenever you feel the need to improve, or work on your nature, that shows distrust within you and unfolds in your actions. When you learn to relax and embrace life, you are allowing nature to flow and unfold through you. There will be ups and downs, but be willing to accept total responsibility for yourself, this puts you in a position of being worthy of receiving and attracting your desires.

Your ego loves to protect itself by bonding with life's wounds and reminding you of how unworthy you are of receiving that which you desire. Learning to let go and forgive is necessary to move forward. Forgiveness is a spiritual act of love for yourself and, when you really live it, sends that message to everyone, including yourself. Forgiveness means that you fill yourself with love and you radiate that love outward, refusing to hang onto feelings of hatred.

Learn to only speak in positive and improvement terms. Make every effort to remove internal habits of pessimism, negativity, judgment, complaints, gossip, cynicism, resentment and fault finding from your vocabulary and inner dialogue. Replace these with optimism, love, acceptance, kindness and peace as your way of processing your environment and people.

Meditate to center yourself to your divine being and remove unproductive, internal dialogue. When you are in turmoil and pre-occupied with winning and defeating, you are at the mercy of your ego, which loves confusion. All of the inner confusion keeps you wondering about yourself and your own value in comparison to others.

Your vision is going to be a precise, clearly defined goal with a detailed plan and timetable for achieving that goal.

1. Write a clear and precise description of the dream.

2. Make a "Goals Page" list for intermediate goals that need to be achieved to fulfill that dream.

3. Make a "goals to steps" list to accomplish intermediate goals.

4. List all tasks to be completed for each goal.

5. Assign completion dates to each task and step.

To add fuel and momentum to your vision, you need to use "hope." I define "hope" as a confident belief that a specific vision (goal, desire, or promise) will be achieved or fulfilled within a specific amount of time. If your vision is too vague you will not be able to sustain enough hope to achieve them. Make your vision as vivid and specific as possible. True hope is knowledge of where you want to go and having a precise map on how to get there. The more you use it to achieve each goal, the more you will have for the next goal on the ladder, building momentum and progress.

"Hope deferred makes the heart sick: but desire fulfilled is a tree of life" Solomon, Proverbs 13:12 (this is why procrastination is destructive)

"Give up too many dreams, and living becomes a little more than just getting by"

People are critical to your vision:

When you make commitments with other people, you instill hope in them. Break those commitments and they will lose hope and trust in you. Learn to help others fulfill their genuine needs and dreams; watch their trust and hope explode and the byproduct will be a new level of creativity to help you and your endeavors.

When lacking hope, ask yourself, "Was it caused by a person breaking a commitment or by me not having a true vision of what I want?"

In order to really get your shine on for the whole world to witness, you must develop that inner shine. Once you begin to develop and trust your inner self, it will shine through and radiate for everyone to see. Then, working on obtaining external desires will be fun, because they are being accomplished from a place that doesn't need to be satisfied from a superficial or ego-based level.

All major religions point that personal fulfillment on earth begins from the inside.

1. Christianity: "The kingdom of heaven is within you"

2. Islam: "Those who know themselves know their god"

3. Buddhism: "Look within you, you are the Buddha"

4. Yoga: "God dwells within you as you"

We are all drawn to people who possess the intangible qualities that attract us to them. These intangible qualities dwell in the realm of that person's spirit and inner self. They have developed faith in themselves to let the inner-self or spirit shine through, unfiltered, for the whole world to see without worrying how people will perceive and judge them. This is how some people who never wish to become famous become famous. Many people desire to feel important and become famous but at some deep level, they don't want to reveal their own special person, because they are afraid of ridicule, which keeps them from achieving their desires.

"Being independent of the good opinion of others and being detached from the need to be right are two powerful indicators that your life is shifting toward a consciousness of trust in yourself and trust in god" **Dr. Wayne Dyer**

When you develop trust in yourself, you are trusting God at the same time. When I speak of "God," take it in whatever form works for you. The important thing is the feelings you associate to the word. For me, God is the infinite universe.

"A human being is a part of the whole, called by us universe, a part limited in time and space he experiences himself, his thoughts and his feelings as something separated from the rest, a kind of optical delusion of his consciousness" – Albert Einstein

Your environment is not something that you must push. It is an extension of yourself, just as you are an extension of the environment. People are classified into two groups. The first group sees itself separate from everyone else believing people can always change. They see everything from a material point of view, and will never be happy, because they will always feel that any experience could have been better. The second group sees itself as a part of the larger whole and trusts in the collective wisdom of the whole. This group is people who are spiritual seekers.

Trust in the wisdom of your feelings. If you feel it, it is true for you. You can avoid being controlled by attitudes that belong to others by not placing your trust in something your heart does not feel.

Creating your reality is nothing more than materializing a new aspect of yourself to which you have always been connected to on a spiritual level. Become aware of how your judgments prevent you from connecting to whatever you are judging. Anytime you catch yourself judging something, you are trying to prove your separateness from it. Remember that it really is possible to look out on the world and not condemn it. You just observe it and allow it to be, don't try and make any interpretation of it.

"Good judgment is a natural expression of wisdom; but it is directly dependent on harmony within, which is peace of mind. When the mind lacks harmony, it has no peace; and without peace it lacks both judgment and wisdom" - Yogananda

Your energy will skyrocket once you notice that you are not judging your environment. Seeing yourself as part of everything might seem impossible to grasp. Try and cultivate the mentality to grasp the ungraspable and you can do that in each moment. Learn to think unconditionally—the conditions, events, and situations that happen in your life appear based on the conditions you set forth. The more you begin to trust your creative abilities, the less you put conditions on how they should happen and become open to infinite possibilities.

"He who sees that the lord of all is ever the same in all that is - immortal in the field of mortality- he sees the truth, and when a man sees that the god in himself is the same god in all that is, he hurts not

18

himself by hurting others, then he goes indeed, to the highest path" -
Bhagavad-Gita

As you read the remainder of this book, remember the following formula
and explore how you can make it happen with the ideas and concepts I
present.

**Your Unique Valuable Contribution + technology, influential
marketing + your niche market + the tools to empower your followers
who will spread your message = FREEDOM**

2 MEDITATION

In today's fast paced modern world, it seems that many have come to find that the one thing that stands between their happiness is not materialistic wants, but their own mind.

We live each day with thousands of things demanding our minds precious attention. We think incessantly about a million things that many of us become slaves to our minds. In fact, we think so much that as soon as we have time to be still, we don't even know how to enjoy being quiet.

The only way you will ever experience peace of mind is by learning to drop the analytical thinking mind. Meditation is a way to help you on the journey of achieving mental clarity and peace. It's time for you to awaken your mind to its potential.

Through mediation you will discover and catch glimpses of a state of consciousness that is truly aware and alert. Meditation will be your tool for deep introspection of your inner being and will prove to be very valuable in your day-to-day life.

It will help you develop an intimate relationship with your true self. As you develop your inner being you will become valuable to those around you, because you will be more in touch to whom you really are. An intimate intuitive knowing beyond any mental conception you have of yourself.

You can only truly help others when you have become the master of your mind, free of false illusions. Many people feel that just because they have the urge to help that they are able to help. Unless you really know what your true identity is, which is not your ego, you will only be trying to offer help from something that is an illusion.

The beauty of proper meditation is that it helps you create immense distance in your inner space. It gives you perspective and your level of consciousness changes. It helps you create distance between your thoughts and the witness who watches your thoughts.

The problem for most is that they remain too close to their thoughts, being close means being identified. This is why psychoanalysis never actually solves the causes of your problems, it may help you function more efficiently in society, but you remain on the same level. Your problem is in your thinking, and you try to solve it with thinking, you still remain within the field of thought.

Meditation gives you vertical growth; it gives you a bird's eye perspective to see your problems, an awareness to freely observe your conditioning. You become an impartial observer, being impartial you will see the causes, you gain understanding. There is no need to solve the problem, you just need more understanding. It simply exists because you lack sufficient understanding, not enough awareness.

That's why we are always able to give someone else great advice, we are far from the problem, we are impartial, we have clarity to see. The person with the problem is too close to it, too identified, he will say, "easy for you to say, this isn't your problem". Meditation helps you create the distance for you to "see" clearly.

Many say that it would be nice to have peace of mind, to learn to be calm no matter what goes on around them. But as long as you make those things objects of your desire, you have already identified yourself as lacking them, thus keeping your "self" from experiencing peace.

When people begin to attempt meditating, they say that it is difficult and boring. When you learn to watch what's going on inside you, if those thoughts of boredom come up, just watch them. Explore why you are telling yourself this is boring, pay attention to your feelings, where is it coming from? There is a huge growing experience hidden, you just need to explore it.

"There are strange moments in life when the mind rests without any kind of worries. When our mind is quiet, when our mind is in silence, then the new arrives."- Samael Aun Weor

Meditation is the act of allowing the thoughts in your mind to cease. When you drop your mind you will experience oneness with the universe. You will realize that everything really is intimately interconnected and multi-dimensional.

The only thing that keeps you thinking you are separate is your body and mind. When you are asleep and disconnect your mind from your body your consciousness is one with the universal consciousness. Mediation is your key in transcending the confines of your body and mind to consciously experience a higher state of universal awareness.

Through a daily discipline of meditation you will become more mindful and calm. Calmness is the ideal state in which you should receive and take part in your life's experiences. Someone who is calm has the mental clarity to handle any situation that life throws at him. Even mindedness should be your goal, learning to maintain a clear-headed mind state helps you with enjoying and dealing with a fast-paced lifestyle.

The more that you focus your attention within, you will begin to feel a new power and new peace rise up within you. Meditation is the ability to stay actively calm. Meditation does not even have to be what many associate meditation with, which is to get into a lotus position and start chanting a mantra.

Any activity that you enjoy can be meditation; you just need to learn to be watchful of whatever you are doing. Learning to be fully present in any activity is meditation. Jogging through the forest and being observant of everything going on inside you without judgment is meditation. It is however important to incorporate a daily routine of meditation and do it earnestly and consistently if you are to reap the rewarding effects.

TOOLS TO CREATE YOUR VISION Visualization Exercises (meditation):

Read the entire section, I will explain why most self-help books fail to produce the results people want.

You can think of meditation as conscious sleeping. Just as you sleep to gain energy for daily functioning, meditation is conscious sleeping that gives you energy (creative abilities) that you need to accomplish goals.

Use the power of meditation to help you achieve your goals. Meditate every day, one minute, each year of your current age. For example, I'm 24, and meditated at least 24 minutes every day. If you are new to meditation, research Vipassana meditation. There are many mediation techniques, so find something that feels good to you.

My Daily Routine

1. Pick a comfortable place to meditate:

Have an intention on what you plan to meditate on beforehand. Ex. A destination you want to visit.

2. Find a comfortable position to sit:

It does not matter if you sit in a chair or on the floor so long as it is comfortable.

3. Cross your legs, clasp your hands together: (this helps make your energy circuit and gives stability.

4. Close your eyes, then stop inner and outer chatter: The more you practice, the better you will get at quieting your mind.

5. Relax, begin thinking that your whole body is becoming extremely relaxed.

6. You will notice that your mind is full of many thoughts:

Your mind will question those thoughts for answers, whether they are known or unknown. This is why your mind (ego) can be your enemy, if it mostly thinks in negative terms, especially if you have thoughts that don't have answers—your mind will rationalize answers that may or may not be true. Remember, we can't see past a choice we don't understand no matter how hard we try.

7. To properly meditate, you need to transcend your mind and thoughts: Your mind and thoughts separate you from your higher self; you can also think of your higher self as your subconscious mind—don't worry about the labels.

8. You transcend your mind by simply observing your breath:

Don't inhale/exhale consciously, just observe your natural breathing and don't force anything. Don't go behind your thoughts, if you catch yourself drifting. Always come back to your breathing. Slowly, the amount of thoughts reduces, and your breathing becomes thinner and shorter. If you focus on your breath, you will get to the point of no thought and no breath. This state of no thinking is your connection to divine being and energy in the body. The more you meditate, the more benefits and energy you will receive.

9. Meditating will give you a pleasurable feeling:

If you feel any discomfort in your body, these can be possible areas of disease or illness. You might heal your body naturally if you meditate every day.

10. Now you are in a state of not thinking and total relaxation. Begin to think only on your intention: Whatever you think now is in a state that will be impregnated directly into your subconscious. It is incredibly important that you don't color any thoughts with lack, limitation, disbelief or doubt. This is why almost all self-help material doesn't produce the results that people expect. Wishing for more money, or anything else, never works; the thought of wanting more money also has the thought of doubt attached to it. So now what you desire and what you think are in conflict and cancel each other out.

Ask yourself how many thoughts and beliefs that you have are modified in a way that is not beneficial to you. You never realize that you are programming your subconscious all day. This is why meditation is so powerful. You are able to make suggestions to your subconscious where the thought is not modified in any way, shape or form. For example, if you want to make things happen fast, you need to eliminate the concept of attaching a timeframe to your thoughts. Everything you receive in life is based on the conditions that you set up, and time is usually one condition that causes the most frustration for people.

Your conscious mind is the gatekeeper for what thoughts you let in. Choose to become more aware and conscious about what you think all day long. Learn to see the world in a non-linear way, remove time from your consciousness, and watch how things arrive in your life faster than you ever thought.

Thoughts = feelings = actions = results (Just like that you can begin to shape your life, become more aware and conscious of your inner dialogue and take control of it)

11. Mentally rehearse every moment of meditation with all your senses: Dare to be like Peter Pan.

12. Visualize in vivid detail, your intention as established fact: Make sure you meditate only on days you feel good. Remember, you want your thoughts to be as pure as possible. This means that you really find out what you want, make sure it's not something you want solely for ego purposes.

Thoughts that involve the ego are usually colored with negativity.

13. With time you will begin to hold vivid pictures of anything:

The third eye, also known as the inner eye, is a metaphysical and esoteric concept referring to the point between your eyes and corresponds to your pituitary glands. It is known as the symbol that leads to spaces of higher consciousness. In Hinduism and Buddhism, the third eye is a symbol of enlightenment. If you are interested, there meditations you can do to awaken your third eye. The more you hold onto an image in your mind, the more power you will give it.

14. Get up and have a great day :) Notice how much energy you have the rest of the day. As you advance in your discipline, you will have a lot of fun creating your day before it starts.

Mantras

The word "mantra" is a Sanskrit word, made up of two root words. "Man," means "mind" or thinking, and "tra," means to "release or free." Therefore, the meaning is to free the mind and thinking from the material sphere of consciousness, thus transcending the physical world. Saints, yogis, Sadhus, and Maharishis have practiced mantra for several thousand years. They are sacred sound vibrations, which contain great spiritual power and energy. Hindus believe that chanting the right mantra can attain God, good health, fortune, and victory over enemies. There are many categories of mantras a few of which include: curing disease; warding off negative planetary influences; thwarting an enemy's actions; distracting enemies, obtaining liberation…" astroved.com

Mantras are a tool to use to change your vibration frequency through the use of the sounds of creation. Find a sound or words that feel good to you.

The words or sounds you say to yourself don't really matter, but the feelings that those words create.

"Everything is possible through the repetition of my mantra. It is more powerful than the atomic bomb" (Om Namah Shivaya) - Babaji

Windows Movie Maker: Another tool I use to keep me motivated, making movies—recorded with music that makes me feel good—with pictures of me doing things I love and am grateful for. My movies are on my iPod so I can easily remind myself of the things I am grateful for. This can really help when you're having a bad day and need to switch your attention in a positive way.

3 DEVELOPING EMPOWERING BELIEFS AND AFFIRMATIONS

To make your vision a reality, you have to adopt beliefs that will help you reach your goals. For example, if you envision retirement on a private beach, but don't believe you can do it, you have already sabotaged yourself. Your desire and belief are in conflict with each other, and you will not manifest what you want in life. When you truly decide to do something, you will find a way to do it.

I also like to think of beliefs as your own ancient proverbs. Cervantes describes proverbs as, "short sentences, drawn from long experiences." By crafting certain beliefs that you want to adopt, they will give you the feeling that you are operating from a level of vast past experiences and wisdom.

Example:

Adopt "Do unto others as you would do unto you," and really live it—watch how you take on a whole new life and identity. You will feel like you skipped years of personal learning experience when you truly live this belief that you have adopted.

Since everything we learn comes back and is interpreted by memory, it's important to have powerful beliefs of oneself. When confronted with a situation, your mind goes to work through a process of deduction from past experiences (memory), and depending on the belief you had, it will impact how you proceed with the present situation. Make internal proverbs for yourself that will be ingrained in your memory to deal with daily encounters.

Example: Beliefs I have made for myself

I believe that, "I can learn anything with the right tools and resources". When I am confronted with a situation where I feel overwhelmed it's as if, like magic, this belief I have pops into my consciousness. Then my mind begins to operate from this level. Then I find myself looking for solutions instead of complaining. Most of the time, I will be able to take proactive actions that lead me to the answer to my problem.

"Nothing happens unless first a dream" – Carl Sandburg

Some Ways to shape your beliefs

1. Always think Success: As soon as you think about failure, forget about it and don't let any negative thoughts snowball. The more attention you give a thought, the more powerful it becomes, and then you will make it harder for yourself to get back to a productive mind state.

The only way to change how you feel is to think about something else. Whenever you feel doubt, fears, and failure creeping into your mind, have a default thought to avoid giving attention to mental poison. As soon as I feel I am entertaining negative thoughts, I immediately think, "My inner-world creates my outer-world." I immediately feel the negativity melt away as I focus on my new positive thought.

2. Develop the belief that you are better than you currently feel: Don't look at your weaknesses as a burden, but as an opportunity to improve yourself. When I find something I don't like about my personality, I don't get down on myself for it, I realize that I have something to work on to make myself better. Most importantly, love and accept who you are, not who you will or should be. Unconditional love for yourself is the only emotion that diffuses negative emotion.

3. Believe that the sky's the limit: If you have little goals, you will have little success. The bigger your dreams, the more potential you will have success. Even If you think your dream is too big, strive to reach that dream, because you will end at a better place than if you set your sights on a smaller goal. The trick is to really believe you can do it. Wishful thinking never got anyone anything, you need to find out what you want and go for it. If you really want that house on the beach your mind will think of ways to get it.

Example: In India, when they are training baby elephants, they tie a small piece of colored rope to their leg to keep them from going anywhere. When the elephants are great big animals, they are so powerful that they can rip a metal chain. But as soon as they put on that brightly colored flimsy rope, the elephant doesn't try to escape, because in its mind, it feels it's impossible to break away. The elephant has become a slave to an idea, which has no basis of truth. I just want you to think of anything that might be limiting you, but you don't question it anymore. Find out if there's really any truth to it by experiencing it for yourself.

How to remove junk beliefs

1. Meditate on your old belief and tell the truth about it:

Now replace it with a belief that will better serve you. Meditate and affirm it until you feel you have changed that belief. The best way is to start acting out your new belief until it becomes a habit, and eventually part of your personality. It usually takes around 30 to 40 days to form a habit. Practice it every day without fail and start all over until you reach at least a month without skipping a single day. This will develop the neural network in your brain for it to become an unconscious part of you.

Now when you accept these beliefs it means you have to raise your standards and develop a strategy that puts you on the road to accomplish what you set forth. Read books that spark interest or help you discover any distinctions that will point you in the right direction. Find a role model, a person who has already accomplished what you want. Find out what some of their beliefs, interests, body language, image, etc. is and adopt them as your own.

Your role model can serve as a blueprint. The goal is to cut down on the trial and error to get where you want faster than you ever thought possible. You can take all the qualities from all the people you admire and add your own personal touch. Thomas Edison is one of the greatest inventors in history, he was able to elaborate, modify and adapt on other's ideas.

You don't have to recreate the wheel just constantly be aware of any success ingredients you come across and make them part of your identity. I am constantly going back to old notebooks with thoughts and ideas that I can put to use. Remember, no idea is stupid, no matter how much you might think it is; it can serve as an allusion to a new idea. Make sure you keep a journal for all your ideas and write them down; you never know when you will use it.

Consistency will develop into habits and this is key because if you fail to be consistent with your actions, you will not be consistent with who you desire to be. A lack of consistency between your actions and what your mind knows you are capable of leads to stress, confusion, and even depression. This is why awareness of self is critical; you need to be constantly evaluating yourself. Decide if the persona you are currently displaying is the reality that you want for yourself, because with enough time that's what your reality will become.

4 RESEARCHING THE WORLD YOU WANT

Once you develop the right mindset, it's time to figure out what world you really want to build for yourself. This is the part that is fun and creative, you only live once and might as well make your perfect world. Make a list of the things that truly matter to you. Think about reasons you listed those items and how to make it reality. This should be the most important research that you will do.

Bear in mind that doing what you love will make the process of making money and attaining the things on your list more pleasurable and easier. It seems simple, but that should not take away from the truth. Your goal is to gain as much knowledge in your area of interest, and it should be that which makes you feel good. If you feel good most of the time, work won't feel like work.

"An expert is a person who has made all the mistakes that can be made in a very narrow field" - Niels Bohr

The purpose of this exercise is to get you excited about the possible things you can have in life and that you can definitely figure out how to get them. You need to break things up into pieces to get a better sense of how to accomplish it. Let go of your fears. It's ok to start in baby steps; the important thing is that you start doing little things that will build momentum in attaining all the worlds that you want. Below is a list of my desires and an example about how I would achieve one of my desires.

My Sample list:

1. Loving Family

2. Financial Freedom

3. Traveling the world

4. Picking up interesting hobbies

5. Beautiful girlfriend or wife

Financial Freedom

Reasons: Many people would love to be rich, but many want it for the wrong reasons, and later find out that money doesn't make them happy. Consider your reasons for financial security with a sincere heart. Some of the reasons I would like to be wealthy are: freedom to pursue anything I want, time to raise my family, ability to travel and learn from different people and cultures, and to give back.

Some things I might do:

1. Start up your own business that you have a passion for. When you work for someone else, your money is taxed at higher rate, but the self-employed writes off legitimate business expenses to absorb the government's taxes on income.

2. Every month put away 10% to 20 % of earnings in a portfolio set up with a financial advisor. I know this sounds easy but hardly anyone does it, because many people are controlled by fear. This fear usually comes from a lack of understanding about how money and investments work. Investing is like learning to drive, once you educate yourself, and with practice, it's easier to do. You will be educated enough to explain your goals and objectives to a financial advisor and knowledge to know if he is doing his job correctly.

3. Invest in Real estate

4. If you have tons of ideas, find out if you can patent your idea and receive royalties, or write a book. Remember, no one sees the world like you; share your perspective.

5. Educate yourself about how money works. Read **"Rich Dad Poor Dad,"** by Robert Kyosaki and the "Richest Man From Babylon".

6. Leverage all the tools you have available to you. We live in a very exciting time; recent advancements have made it possible for the little guy to leverage resources that only a few years back was not accessible. A great book to get you thinking about great ideas to leverage technology is "The 4 Hour Work Week" by Tim Ferris.

7. If being an entrepreneur is not your cup of tea, the resources below can be a great alternative. Many companies have chosen to increase productivity by outsourcing jobs to people who want to work from home. All that is needed is an Internet connection and the discipline to be productive from home. If you do your homework, you will find a way to build up your financial future.

If you find something that you love and that your good at, research the way to make money, no matter what it is you would like to do, you just have to want it bad enough and be creative enough to make it work. I will help you come up with a plan on how to use technology to find creative ways to make a living doing what you enjoy. If you are not really the entrepreneur type but would love to work from home, you will find resources below on how it can be done.

Leveraging technology to leverage your time, location, and occupation

Flexible Jobs and Companies:

www.tentilltwo.com

www.flexjobs.com

www.aquent.com

www.part-timeprofessionals.com

www.momcorps.com

www.ivyexec.com

Advice:

www.escapefromcubiclenation.com

www.familiesandwork.com

www.telecommuting.com

Job Boards:

www.hotjobs.com

www.careerbuilder.com

www.sologig.com

www.monster.com

www.indeed.com

www.simplyhired.com

www.guru.com

www.elance.com

www.idealist.org

www.craigslist.com

www.backpage.com

www.mediabistro.com

Telephone based Customer Service Agents:

www.telereach.com

www.intrep.com

Medical Transcription, Coding and Billing:

www.medquist.com

www.precysesolutions.com

Online Tutoring Services:

www.tutor.com

www.kaplan.com

www.esylvan.com

www.brainfuse.com

www.growingstars.com

www.smarthinking.com

Virtual Assistant:

www.assistu.com

www.getfriday.com

www.vanetworking.com

www.teamdoubleclick.com

www.charmcityconcierge.com

Home Based Virtual Customer Service Agents:

www.aplineaccess.com

www.liveops.com

www.arise.com

www.west.com

www.workingsolutions.com

Resources for Writers:

www.author101.com

www.writersmarket.com

www.wellfedwriter.com

www.fundsforwriters.com

www.worldwidefreelance.com

www.adsolutewrite.com

www.myessays.com

www.writerfund.com

www.payperpost.com

www.bloggingads.com

Translation Services:

www.welocalize.com

www.telelanguage.com

www.sdl.com

www.accurapid.com

Crafting Services:

www.scrapbook.com

www.ebay.com

www.cashcrafters.com

www.etsy.com

Website help:

www.1and1.com

www.blogger.com

www.pages.google.com

www.godaddy.com

www.text-link-ads.com

www.elance.com

www.guru.com

Organizational Expertise:

www.napo.net

www.orderfromchaos.com

Support:

www.support.com

www.geeksontime.com

www.geeksquad.com

www.plumchoice.com

www.supportfreaks.com

When you have identified a specific world, make it an efficient process:

1. Knowing what you don't want to experience.

2. Identifying only what you do want to experience.

3. Clear any limiting beliefs that you might currently have right now. When you think of your African safari, do you feel 100 percent that you will make it happen? Analyze how you feel, and if there's any doubt, explore those feelings. Why do you feel like this?

4. Create experiences that give you a taste of what you want so you know how it feels. Say you want a Porsche, how do you really know you want one, unless you know how it feels. Rent one for a day, you might even surprise yourself and find out that the idea of having a Porsche was more compelling than actually having one.

5. Let go, create the consciousness that you do not become attached to your desires. Becoming attached to your desires will cause you to hold them away from you. Have faith and confidence in knowing that if it's really a part of your higher purpose, you will have it in the future.

While you wait for your desires to manifest, start today to work towards that vision by practicing the right attitude—begin dressing it, talking it, acting it, and living it.

5 MAKING AND INFLUENCING FRIENDS

"Any fool can criticize, condemn, and complain - and most fools do, but it takes character and self-control to be understanding and forgiving" - Dale Carnegie

How fast you reach your goals depends on how well you deal with people and the level of influence you have on them. If you are ever to succeed in business and in life you need to have the ability to network, because that is the essence of business.

In order to really influence people, you must become a person who is likeable. How do you become likeable? You must have a sincere interest in others. Every person on this earth wants to feel important, so you need to treat everyone with respect, because they deserve it. Remember no one is better than you and you are not better than anyone, we are all human beings who deserve the same amount of respect.

Becoming Likeable: Setting the Stage

You should be the first to initiate and set the stage for conversation. Most people are hesitant to be the first—don't be, step out of your comfort zone.

If you are shy, this can be one of the hardest things to do, but the more you do it, the more you condition yourself for it to become second nature. As a small child I used to be really shy, but I noticed that outgoing children tended to be happier, so I stepped out of my comfort zone, and today I can walk up to almost anyone.

This is going to take time; things don't happen overnight but don't let this discourage you. Many people feel that it takes five years to become proficient in something. Don't waste any time, start today and each day after that will get easier. Each different experience will later serve as a reference to remind you, that you can approach almost anyone.

The first person to initiate conversation has a certain degree of control. Have you ever noticed how persuasive people can seduce you to their ways, dictating your body language and basically synchronizing it to theirs? This is because people naturally imitate other people as a way of communicating with the other person.

If the person you are approaching appears sad, approach them with a big confident smile. More than likely, they will smile; you will automatically change their mood and increase chances to have a better conversation. With time you will be able to catch all the subtleties a person gives off and use that to set the stage for meaningful communication.

This will require you to have an open mind and immerse yourself in as many different worlds and cultures as possible. That's why I have friends from various backgrounds—people who are skaters, basketball players, artists, musicians, writers, and more. These friendships helped me to quickly learn about their worlds and relate to many people who are different from me.

By knowing what kind of stage to set up you will know how to get the other person to think very highly of you. For example, by being observant you will catch the subtleties in the way a person appears to be—the way he is dressed, body language, tone of voice, language, etc.—which will help you to imagine placing yourself in their shoes. This will help you read how the person is feeling, thereby an idea of what approach to use when trying to communicate effectively.

When I pick up subtleties, I will know what topics, questions, and general interests appeal to the person, giving me information to win that person as a friend. For example, if know Mike is passionate about cars, I will ask a question about cars with the minimum knowledge I have.

"The Deepest urge in the human nature is the desire to be important" - Dale Carnegie

Now you set the stage for Mike who will love to tell me exactly why the Mitsubishi EVO is better. When someone is knowledgeable about something it's in their nature to tell you, because it is one more opportunity for them to show how great or smart, they are. You have to cater to their ego and never test or contradict their ideas. They will not accept someone, who is supposed to know less, tell them they are possibly wrong. If I told him that I heard that the Subaru WRX is better, we would have just gotten in an argument that he would not have backed out of. In an argument, no one wins, even if you are technically correct. Even if you get your point across, why does that matter? Remember, you're trying to make a new friend, don't make a bad impression.

Your likeability factor is going to come down to:

Your presence: What you look like, how you dress, how you move, etc.

Your attitude: Your attitude will determine the quality of your thoughts, your voice tone, words, and most importantly, your facial and body language. It will influence what you are saying, how you are saying it, and how interesting you are perceived to be. Your attitude is going to determine how people respond and connect with you. Be aware of the type of attitude that you should be displaying given your environment.

Some good attitudes to have: enthusiastic, warm, relaxed, welcoming, interested, confident, laid back. Think about when you meet someone who is extremely confident, they make you feel confident by just being in their presence. With time you will also become confident, if confident people constantly surround you. This is why it is important who you choose to spend your time with. Over time we all adopt the attitudes of the people around us. Choose to be the one who constantly uplifts and makes people feel comfortable by the attitude you practice.

Attitudes you should stay away from: anger, impatience, afraid, mocking, rude, disrespectful, anxious, pessimistic, conceited, self-conscious.

How you make people feel: Are you able to get people to engage in certain feelings that will make communication more meaningful.

People who vouch for you: Are you meeting new people through your friends? If so, they will already have expectations of what kind of person you are from what your friends have told them about you. If you meet their expectations, or even exceed them, you will be able to make meaningful connections very quickly.

Body Language

Whenever you approach someone for the very first time, your body language will do most of the talking and the other person will make an immediate first impression of you. Always be aware that whatever you say, your body is also in agreement. If you say one thing and your body says the opposite, you will appear to be a fake person. We have all seen the girl that walks up to another girl and says, "I'm so happy to see you. How you been? You look so good," but their body language is saying, "What are you doing here? I'm not really listening to what you're saying." This is easily seen and can be one of the rudest things you can do when making new friends.

Always approach someone with open gestures and a smile. If you approach someone with crossed arms, this will automatically make the other person defensive and question your motives. Smiling is infectious; if the other person has a stern look on their face the moment you approach them with a smile, you will gradually notice that they will smile too. This usually sets up for a good conversation, because both people are in good moods. Try this: If you're in a neutral mood right now, put a big smile on your face. Pay attention. You can feel your body changing and your mood immediately start to change. People who are in good moods place more importance on what you have to say. When you are congruent with your actions people will begin to trust you and give you a better chance of being liked and building rapport.

Questions and Listening

Your next goal is to sincerely find out as much as you can about the person. Ask quality questions; find out what is important to the person—their goals, beliefs, interests, etc.

The key is to be sincere, so the person feels comfortable and more likely to open up. Your goal is to find common ground to help establish rapport with the person.

Try to have a calm demeanor; refrain from being overly eager as this might scare or turnoff the other person. Try to not be overly polite, don't smile too hard, and try not to be patronizing. You must adapt to the mood of the person. You can do this by being observant to the visual, verbal, and vocal clues they give you and then synchronizing yourself to them. If the person is excited to tell you a story, you must become excited as well and mirror that back to them visually, verbally, and vocally. If the person is telling you a sad story, you must show sincere empathy. Be open-minded and really listen to the person.

"If you want to relate well to others, you have to be willing to focus on what they have to offer."

Synchronizing Tips

--Tilting and nodding your head: When done properly, it tells the person that you are paying attention.

--Facial Expressions: Open friendly expressions show agreement and understanding. Closed constricted facial expressions show confusion and frustration.

--Breathing: Pay attention to the rhythm of their breathing. Try and synchronize with their breathing, this makes you feel like you are on the same wavelength as the other person.

--Tone: Try and feel the emotions of the other person, so that you can emit the same tonality.

--Volume: Is the person loud or quiet? Adjust your volume so that it matches the person.

--Speed: Does the person speak slow or fast? Someone who is a slow talker will feel uncomfortable speaking with a fast talker.

--Words: What type of words or slang is the person comfortable with? Knowing this can be very powerful in getting some to feel at ease with you.

Listening

Listen twice more than you talk. Listening requires more than pretending to listen or simply hearing a person talk. Listening and hearing are two completely different things and the person can tell if you're really listening to them, or simply hearing them speak Being a good listener is a skill, you must become an active listener. It's all about the other person, who cares if you don't get to talk about yourself.

If you're an effective listener, you will gain a better understanding of that person's thoughts, perspectives, feelings and actions. Take this as an opportunity to become more persuasive and influential.

The problem with most people is that listening doesn't have much value to them. They feel that in order to get people to like them they must do a great deal of the talking. When you meet someone for the first time you are completely foreign to them. People are usually not interested in things they don't understand, and that includes you. To get someone to be interested in knowing you, you must first talk about things that interest them. As soon as they feel that you understand or relate to them, they will become more curious about getting to know you too.

Think about that for a minute, how do you like it when another person is talking so much that when you try and say something they keep talking. You eventually quit listening to that person because you got too annoyed. Sometimes you don't need to do most of the listening; you constantly need to evaluate the situation. Sometimes people really want to hear what you have to say. In this situation, turn the question around on them to get them involved. Below are the pros and cons for those who talk too much versus those who are sincere listeners.

People who talk too much

1. People always talk about them behind their backs

2. In group settings they feel they always need to say something just to feel like they are contributing.

3. Usually have very big egos.

4. They ask questions that they already have the answers to.

5. They aren't even listening to what someone is saying, because they are too focused on having something to say

People Who Listen Effectively

1. Get the whole picture, and then act accordingly.

2. Everyone loves a good listener so you will make tons of friends.

3. No one talks bad about you, who ever said, "Man that kid just loves to listen too much."

Good listening is going to really take effort. The reason is that people can think faster than they speak. You begin to think of other things as that person is speaking. Then you become consumed with those thoughts. Next thing you know, the other person asks you "So, do you think I did the right thing?" You weren't listening so you have no idea what to say. This is one of the biggest turnoffs.

Things to keep in mind during a conversation:

--Focus on understanding

--Sum up at major intervals

--Ask questions for clarity

--Suspend your judgment

--Look at the speaker

Paraphrasing

Paraphrasing, when done properly, can advance your relationship with the speaker. The key is to listen empathetically. Paraphrasing lets the speaker know that you are processing what he has to say and lets him know your point of view on what he has said. This also makes the speaker feel reassured that you are trying to understand their thoughts and feelings, and many people will really appreciate that. The main reason of why paraphrasing can be very powerful is that if you are able to get to the bottom of the person's reasoning, you will be one step closer to being a person of influence to them.

Example:

"Ok Mary, let me get this straight. I understand what you are saying. You told Matt no, because you were afraid of what your parents would think."

"That's exactly it. Jane, I really appreciate that you really listen to me and try and understand my situation."

Things to avoid when listening: Don't Interrupt

Because you have the upper hand by thinking faster than someone who is speaking, you will be tempted to interrupt. Don't, because the other person will get the feeling that you don't care what they are saying. The other person might also have great momentum telling you a story, but when you interrupt them, their story doesn't carry as much feeling when they start speaking again. You also show that you enjoy speaking more than being a good listener. When you interrupt you are also making assumptions of what you think the other person is about to say. You risk the other person losing interest to continue telling you their story.

Don't finish people's sentences

This can be very rude, and you take a gamble on guessing where the person is going. Be patient. Let them collect their thoughts and convey their message the way they want to.

Don't offer advice to soon

Listen to the entire story so you can offer your perspective on the situation. Be cautious, because many people already know what they need to do. The important thing is that they just wanted someone to listen and have an opportunity to vent their feelings, be it good or bad.

Compliments + Appreciation

The way to make people feel important is through sincere compliments and appreciation.

Most people go out of their way to get other people to notice them, yet many don't. Get in the habit of noticing the little things about people. The little things are what matter and make a person unique—pay attention. Next time you see them, be the first to give them a sincere compliment on something even as simple as their hair cut. By making other people feel good about themselves, you should also feel good for doing it—a win-win situation.

Appreciation

Many times people think others owe them something. Nobody owes you anything. Whenever anybody does something for you, show your appreciation and let them know you don't take anything for granted. Be spontaneous; get the person a small gift when they don't expect it.

Encouragement

Once you find out what is truly important to someone, you must provide encouragement. Everyone has dreams and aspirations. Be the one who encourages them to pursue their goals. Any insight or information that's empowering boosts their confidence. Most people are so afraid of failure that they will not pursue their goals. They will give you all the reasons why their goals are out of reach.

Your goal should be to switch their focus on the negative reasons to show how they can make it happen. Whatever we focus on becomes our reality, so when you focus only on the negative aspects, that's all you will see. When they give you a reason why they can't do it, ask them if that's really a reason or a mere excuse. If they are excuses, show them how destructive this mental state is.

One of the best feelings you will get in dealing with people is when you get another person excited about his goals or ideas. Now that the person is excited, you need to point them in the right direction. Help them research the world they want to be in; find out as much relevant information. Help them create a plan and deadlines to reach their goals. Start with small attainable goals, this will help them gain momentum and move on to more challenging goals. By being active in the whole process you will build a deeper and more influential relationship with that person. He will not see you as an associate but as an ally in their journey to success. You will see that for most people it's not what they are that holds them back, it's what they think they're not.

If you know in advance that you will be in a social setting, clear your mind and make a statement aloud, or in your head, about what you hope to experience.

1. State intent: to meet and get to know some interesting people.

2. Create intrigue and rapport through my quality questions and listening.

3. If I feel that I've made a connection with someone, exchange contact information.

Plan and Organize Social Events

One of the best ways to develop a meaningful experience with someone is through a social event. Whenever you participate in an event or trip, your relationship with those people will become even greater. When I studied abroad in Prague, I have never developed such strong relationships in such a short amount of time. I met people from all over the world and on the weekends we would take trips to other countries. On these trips I made incredible bonds, because everyone was on an adventure of experiencing new things together. Experiences are always magnified with more people involved.

Story Telling

Story telling has the ability to make a lasting impression on the people you meet. We have all been conditioned to love and remember stories. Learn how to lead and capture the imagination, because that is the structure to every good story. When people talk about you, it will be in the form of a good memorable story. Learn how to do it in different settings and mediums that is appropriate for your audience.

Resources:

National Story Telling Festival (www.storytellingcenter.com)

Bay area storytelling festival (bayareastorytelling.org)

Digital Storytelling Festival (www.dstory.com)

For College Students

If you're a college student planning events and parties is one of the best ways to be known on campus. Watch the movie National Lampoon's "Van Wilder." You can have that lifestyle if you choose to, and it will be even better because it will be your life. If you apply some of the ideas I present about developing yourself, your college experience will be very fulfilling for the following reasons:

1. You will have hundreds of friends and know thousands of people.

2. You always have something to do because everyone invites you to go out.

3. Because you know so many people, eventually you will see people you know that work at places you eat at on campus and they will hook you up with free things. I remember one time I was on campus getting a slice of pizza. I was in a huge line, but one of the kids working recognized me from my party and told me to skip the line and go straight to the front; I also got a free slice. This is one of the perks of when people have a great time with you; they will do what they can to show their appreciation.

4. If you're a guy, girls find it very attractive because you have so many friends and they wonder why everyone likes you. Your male status is automatically raised.

Becoming more influential with People

Always be aware of your internal dialogue, don't judge people, and always have a healthy social-friendly internal dialogue. People will see you as a charismatic person, because you are keeping your ego in check by constantly monitoring your internal dialogue.

--Don't make assumptions

--Don't take anything personal, be free of criticism (this is a quality that great leaders and influential people possess)

--Be free of fear

--Be impeccable with your word. Say what you mean and mean what you say.

--Give total attention to someone. The best way is with your eyes. Be careful not to look around, or you will think of ways to end the conversation.

Whenever you are communicating with someone, make eye contact with them and as you do, focus on the divine and beautiful person inside them; it is as if you have an amazing transfer of positive energy. If you pay enough attention, you will see that you are more likely to elevate someone's mood.

Influence

Even if you don't see yourself as an influential person, we all influence the people in our lives on some level. Some people are born with very influential qualities, but influence is something anyone can learn and improve on. People observe, contemplate, draw conclusions, and act upon the information given. This is important to know from the perspective of influence, because if you really want to influence someone on a deep level, you eventually have to change the way they behave. If you want to change the way they behave, you have to change the way they think.

Each day try to expand your self-image by seeing yourself and acting as someone who is influential. Before you try to influence someone or something to change, you have to decide what it is that you need to change to have your desired outcome. Once you really become observant, you will find that by changing a few critical behaviors will often lead to major changes with less effort.

When faced with a number of possible options, search for strategies that focus on specific behaviors. When you find the exact behavior that needs to be changed to have the desired outcome, you will know what you need to motivate and enable people to achieve change.

In your daily life, when you are confronted with situations where you would like to become more influential, get in the habit of contemplating on this question, "What must people actually do?"

You need to shift your perspective from focusing on outcomes to focusing and becoming aware of specific behaviors. The main problem with trying to exert influence on the outcomes is that what you actually need to do is unknown. It doesn't matter what you think you need to do to get someone to see things from your point of view. We all make decisions based on our own processes; your goal is to find out how a person makes his decisions, and then influence the behavior that is associated with it.

It is critical to find specific behaviors that will achieve the desired outcome. By being very observant of patterns and how people react to their environment you can discover a few important behaviors, and if you leverage them you will accomplish your intention. By increasing your awareness, all five senses, and developing a mindset that is always scanning for specific behaviors, you will be able to proceed with more information and act accordingly.

Example: I love to play poker, and when I am really focused I try to have an open attitude to always be aware of my surroundings and how it relates to everyone. Finding players with specific behaviors and patterns helps me to read my opponents. If I can influence the behavior without the player knowing, I will throw them off their game. That's why constantly evaluating your image and switching gears is important in case you become predictable in your actions.

By changing specific behaviors, values, attitudes, the desired outcome will follow. The trick is identifying those behaviors. This is where a mentor or role model plays a vital role. If you desire to be like someone, identify the key behaviors the person demonstrates and take action. I have always been interested in being the chief executive officer of my own company, and I met my mentor, Debra Benton, during college. Debra coaches some of the Top CEO's in the country. She wrote, "How to Think like a CEO" and "CEO Material: How to Be a Leader in Any Organization." Through my relationship with her, I had a deeper understanding for the type of thinking that is needed to manage Fortune 500 Company.

The more your level of influence grows the easier it is for you to realize your ideas. If you can identify the behaviors that are best suited for any situation and take focused action, your probability for success skyrockets.

6 SPREADING AND DEVELOPING YOUR IDEAS

In a digital world that provides faster, more efficient ways to retrieve specific information, being creative, unique, and original become increasingly important. Technology brings the whole world to your fingertips. If you are able to let your own voice shine through and be fearless in sharing your ideas, thoughts, and feelings you have all the resources necessary to find an audience.

In Malcolm Gladwell's phenomenal book, "Tipping Point," he describes three types of people that are necessary to spread ideas for a global epidemic. The first type is a connector who knows everyone and everyone knows him. Connectors are also usually trendsetters and don't conform to the norm. Connectors help spread and influence ideas and concepts and have many friends. In chapter 9, I will help you develop your own style that will help you become a trendsetter.

Connectors:

1. If you keep growing and developing yourself, you will be a trendsetter and never conform to the norm, because you're constantly evolving.

2. You have many friends and many people that like you. They also value your opinion and trust you.

The second person is the salesman who has the ability to sell you his ideas through his persuasive personality. Some people have the natural ability of just being able to talk themselves through anything. One of my favorite characters that portray this ability is Vince Vaughn in the Movie "Wedding": and "Old School".

Salesman:

1. Verbal persuasion is their main tool to influence others.

2. Enthusiasm is key to selling ideas to someone.

The third person is the maven who is the know it all.

Maven:

1. The maven will tell you all the pros and cons for anything you research.

2. The maven is very detailed and technical oriented.

One of my goals is to help you be at least two of the three personality types, and you will have access to the one you are missing by having so many friends. If you're a connector and a salesman, you should find a maven who can be a friend, or someone to be your business partner, to help take care of details in your ideas. Get to know your friends' talents. Identify all the connectors, salesman, and mavens within your network. These should be the people you focus on the most to support your ideas, because it will be the most effective. Think of the famous 80/20 rule: 80 percent of results come from only 20 percent of a focused input. Work smarter not harder.

Tools to use with your salesman, maven, and connector

Twitter.com can be a very powerful tool that allows you to develop a relationship with people who are interested in following you. It can be a great way to find your salesman, connectors, and mavens who already have a huge following. Think of Twitter as AOL instant messenger, but instead of one-on-one communication, it is one to many. You can send updates through text messaging, which makes it easy to stay in touch with your followers. The goal is to build a relationship with your followers by keeping them updated with your life. A typical twitter update called a "tweet" can be as simple as, "Ivan is currently reading a good book and eating Ben and Jerry's Ice Cream."

If you are interested in email marketing and copywriting for the Web, follow Kenneth Yu on Twitter. He is someone I have met on the site and has already been valuable to me by exposing me to new ideas through his articles on blog.mindvalleylabs.com.

Touchgraph.com is a visual tool to discover relationships within your friends and ideas.

Squidoo.com is a medium that, if used properly, can enable your followers to spread your message to a huge audience.

Flickr.com can be used creatively to spread your message through pictures.

Stumbleupon helps you discover new sites based on your interests and find a community of like-minded people who can help spread your message.

Tumblr.com is a social network where you can easily share your photos, thoughts, and videos to the world and the people you want to influence.

friendfeed.com consolidates your social media feeds into one site where people can keep track of all the types of media you are involved with.

Google Trends and Compete.com help you discover trends among your market and competitors.

Creating your own tipping point

Start by asking, in order for me to spread my idea, what must people actually do that is congruent with my vision?

Identify specific behaviors to influence your salesman, connectors, and mavens and the people you want to influence.

Take consistent action to achieve your outcome. Create a daily to-do list of tasks that you need to do to spread your message.

Sample Daily To-Do List: Spreading your message on the Web

1. Choose your top five online forums that suit your goals the best. Make a few meaningful posts to each site. Make sure that everything you post is of practical value.

2. Build a List of Bloggers who best represent your message and contribute to their blog by giving valuable feedback on their blog posts. You can search for potential bloggers on technorati.com, which is essentially a search engine for the top blogs on the web.

3. Write One Article for your Blog. If you are not sure how to set up a blog,

check out Wordpress.org. Word press is the easiest state of the art platform to build and maintain your blog. You can also hire someone to set up, design, and upload your site for a relatively inexpensive price. Check out elance.com to have freelancers bid on your job posting.

4. Track RSS feeds from your favorite sites to stay updated with the latest news. RSS feeds can be a great way to brainstorm topics to discuss on your blog and Twitter. To make your job easier of managing your feeds use a free service like Netvibes.com.

5. Write an article and submit to sites like ezinearticles.com or use an article submission service like articlemarketer.com. Articles can be a great way to attract consistent, long-term targeted traffic to your site.

6. Create a Video that supports your message and submit to YouTube.com. You can use a tool like Tubemogul.com to simultaneously submit your videos to many video sites.

7. Use all the different social media and book marking sites like delicious.com, digg.com, furl.net, newsvine.com , Slashdot.org, reddit.com, diigo.com , spurl.net, backflip.com, google bookmarks, fark.com, technorati.com , ma.gnolia.com, netvous.com, hubpages.com, squidoo.com, feedburner.com to enable your audience to easily spread your idea, website, article, etc.

Use social media to your advantage

The corporate media has essentially lost their monopoly on controlling ideas. We live in very exciting times because of the emergence of the new social media technologies. Social media is very important and relevant because no matter what your interest, you can be sure to find large groups of people just like you who are eager to connect and share information. If you are able to make a meaningful contribution to an online community, they in return will be very powerful spokespeople in their circle of influence.

Your ultimate goal in social media is to develop a following of people who look to you for their information and interpretation of the topics of interest. Report and interpret ideas that are valuable and engaging to your audience. Many people on the Internet are finding success through their personal blogs in accomplishing this.

Treat your followers with respect and have a genuine interest in contributing something that will uplift them. In the beginning, continually give without worrying what's in it for you. Once you've gained trust, slowly introduce new ideas and they will have a higher chance of acceptance. Through this process you can educate and prime people to be more understanding of you and your message.

People don't equate hearing something multiple times from multiple sources as an attempt to persuade; they simply see it as mounting evidence that something is true. That's why the Web is so great, because you can have your message circulating through many mediums such as articles, video's, blogs, presentations, pod casts, email, etc. The more your followers hear your message from several sources the more credibility it gains. Have your business card and your "elevator pitch" ready.

How to get people to change their minds

Creating an actual experience that supports your message is the best way to get people to change their minds. If it is not possible to create an experience for someone, your next best option is a vicarious experience, meaning, if a person doesn't learn from doing it himself the next best way is to observe someone else who does it.

What you think doesn't matter rather it's what your audience thinks of you. Their thinking process involves a lot of mini cause and effect scenarios. Find out what they think about you. If it's not what you want it to be, you will need to change their maps of cause and effect.

When altering behavior, you need to help the people you want to persuade to answer two questions:

--Is this going to be worth it? If not, why waste the time and effort. People need to understand the benefits before making a decision. If you create the right compelling benefits that suits the individual, you will get cooperation.

--Can they do it? If you can't show them that they can, why would they want to try? Learn to create teaching methods around how your followers learn best. Do they learn best through their auditory, visual, or kinesthetic faculties, or a combination of all of them?

If you learn to see the world through other's eyes with those questions in mind, you will receive many ideas from them about how to structure your ideas. In the last chapter I will give you an exercise to do just that.

Story Telling to Create a Vicarious Experience

Words and how you say them are some of the most basic ways in which we try to win someone to our way of thinking. It's important to know what words mean to each person, because everyone will have a different interpretation on the same word. When you are seen as someone with integrity, people trust both your knowledge and motives and will become open to your suggestions. When it comes to deeply ingrained beliefs, verbal persuasion rarely works.

I am sure you have had the experience of trying to forcefully get someone to see things the way you do and noticed that they did not listen to what you had to say. The whole time they are looking for every error in your logic and mistake in your facts. Since everything is based off their beliefs and perspective, you lose every time.

A great way to penetrate initial resistance is through realistic stories dealing with real life issues. Then, defenses will lower, and the person will empathize. One tactic is educating someone through entertainment, because it requires participation and changes perspectives on how we interact with the world. Your goal as an influencer is to emulate powerful and emotional real-life experiences. Many commercials on television do a great job of telling stories and evoking strong emotional responses. The challenges you will encounter with storytelling is that the moment that people realize your goal is to convince them of something, you will get resistance.

The reason that a carefully crafted story is so powerful is that it gets the person involved on such a deep level that it transcends their logic and arguments. They go from the role of critic to participant when the story is concrete and vivid.

Motivation

Finding a way to encourage others to both understand and believe in a new point of view may not be enough to propel him into action. In order for someone to take the desired action, their emotions will need to be involved. Just think about when you go shopping, are you buying based on a logical decision or on your emotions? Good advertisers get you to feel a strong emotion and connect it to what they are selling as the solution to your feelings.

Getting someone emotionally involved is accomplished through providing hope in your story and offering a solution for what they need to do. If enough hope is provided people will do the necessary research and take action. If you find yourself confused about why your idea is not clicking with people, the people may not have the necessary knowledge in order to interest them. If something seems like common sense to you, your audience might not have the knowledge necessary to get it. Do your research and find where that disconnect exists.

When trying to communicate an idea, be aware of the visual elements you are exuding (dress, body language, tone of voice). If the signals you are giving off are loud or contrary to your message, your efforts could be worthless. If you look like you just rolled out of bed or you have a hot pink T-shirt, your audience will be so focused on those images that your message will go in one ear and out the other.

One of the best ways to set up an appealing image is through effective questioning. Your goal is to have people express their deepest desires. Then you need to ask questions that revolve around what is important about their desire, so you can set up the emotional appeal.

Steps to create emotional appeal

1. Identify the emotions you are appealing too.

2. Create vivid word pictures that point to the emotions.

3. Ask powerful questions so the audience puts itself in the picture to

experience what they are or would be feeling.

4. Suggest what they are feeling and acknowledge it. This creates a feeling of credibility and trust.

5. Encourage them to feel more of that emotion and link it back to you.

Your niche market won't get your idea unless:

The first impression compels them to look further and research. Use good design principles to capture someone's attention through promotional material.

--Contrast: This is often the most important visual attraction on a page. The elements—type, color, size, line thickness, shape, and space, should look different.

--Repetition: Repeat visual elements of the design throughout the piece. You can repeat color, shape, texture, spatial relationships, line thickness, sizes, etc. This helps develop the organization and strengthens the unity.

--Alignment: Nothing should be placed on the page arbitrarily. Every element should have some visual connection with another element on the page. This creates a clean, sophisticated, fresh look.

--Proximity: Items relating to each other should be grouped close together. When several items are in close proximity to each other, they become one visual unit rather than several separate units. This helps organize information and reduces clutter.

Grabbing Attention

Surprising people automatically gets them to pay attention, because it is a biological response. You need to do it unexpectedly, making sure it supports your idea or message. If you create curiosity in your audience and cause a knowledge gap you need to fill it, or they will, and it might not have the desired outcome. Keep in mind that before you arouse curiosity and open the gaps, you need to understand how you will close them. First, people must realize that they need the facts. This is where influence and a little gentle persuasion help. You need to highlight some specific knowledge that they are missing.

Shift your thinking from "what information do I need to convey" to "what questions do I want my audience to ask." Get to know your audience— their motivations, interests, habits, and beliefs. If you can make a connection and relate to them, any message you are trying to convey will get them to care about their knowledge gaps. If you know the specific questions they have, you can create your response around those questions.

If you want people to act quickly to your ideas, you need to focus on affecting their short-term memory. You can do this through repetition combined with emotional urgency to propel them into the desired action. This will work with the people who may have an immediate need for your message.

Idea Strategy

1. Identify the outcome you want from your actions. The more specific you get, the easier it will be to come up with ideas that will help get desired results.

2. Figure out which memories you need to trigger in your audience to cause them to take action. You will need to do some research.

Other tips

Create events for your followers

Outdoor events like festivals and conventions can be a great way for your followers to meet. Red Bull energy drink does a great job of getting its followers together through their Flugtag events. If you want to persuade the masses you simply create events for them to be around people who feel the same way and can discuss their ideas. This is what politicians are great at doing with their presidential campaigns and conventions.

Creating beliefs in your audience

Simply build on existing beliefs and help them make a connection to the new idea.

Create an event where they can experience your message with a high emotional impact. Musical festivals are great because everyone is consumed with the good vibes of the music and all you have to do is add in your message.

Let people perceived as experts deliver the information that will lead them to accept a new idea.

Reduce your message to the most important component and deliver it with intensity and passion. You don't need to complicate things, keep it simple, and focus on making a meaningful connection.

Repeat the message regularly and from different sources so that it becomes well accepted. Everyone knows Barack Obama's message because it is simple and is repeated regularly.

Use social proof so that new believers become true believers. They will than see that they are part of a group that sees things the same way. If you need to use a celebrity for social proof, try using:

www.contactanycelebrity.com

www.celebbrokers.com

www.celebrityendorsement.com

Acknowledge and appreciate your followers by recognizing their efforts.

Give them methods to display their affiliation with you. A great example of this was Lance Armstrong and Nike's "live strong" wristband.

Give exclusive access to your members: People love to feel like they are special.

You might be able to send out a special email with information that is only available to your members.

Whenever you have a large group of people that you influence, they will begin to derive a sense of self around your idea. Gene Simmons has done a great job of doing this with his hardcore fans. So, it is very important that you create a powerful ideal, which they can connect with. Growing up putting on a pair of Michael "Air" Jordan's tennis shoes made me feel like I would be able to jump higher. Sure, they were nice shoes, but the ideal was larger than life and made me believe in the ability to jump higher.

Building your tipping point followers

1. Create an ideal that is bigger than you and your product. It should be something that people feel proud representing. You also have to make sure that it's something they feel they can carry out.

2. Create an event and make it very public. Then you need to acknowledge your audience as the ones responsible for the success of the event.

3. Educate your followers: once your group gains momentum, it's important to keep that momentum going with ongoing information of where you're headed and how they can become involved.

4. Make sure it's fun so that when you create other events, they will bring their friends to the next event.

5. Document your event and post it on your Web site and other marketing materials.

6. Make them realize the benefits they might have gained from being a part of your community.

7. Help them by giving them means of communicating with other members. Set up a forum or message board on your Web site.

Enthusiasm

When trying to create a brand you should also spend time developing your own vocabulary or tag lines that people connect with. It will be a specific language that your audience can use as a way to identity and connect with one another. Musicians and rappers like Sean Carter a.k.a. "Jay-Z" did a great job of accomplishing this on a global scale. Research your target audience and try to understand how they see themselves. Design a vocabulary the represents those beliefs.

One of my future projects is continuing a clothing line I created during college with my friends called, "Woodside". Our Tag Line was **"Move with the Revolution."**

During college, one of my best friends told me about an idea to start up a clothing company called, "Woodside." Being a person who never passes up an opportunity, I jumped on it immediately. I had no idea what you needed to do to start a clothing company, but I didn't worry about that. So, we got the ball rolling, we had our vision and the purpose for our company, but the problem was that neither of us was a fashion designer or graphic design artist. I began to think as a fashion designer and see the world as they do.

One day I went into a local coffee shop where I met one of my best friends and future business partner. After a small conversation, I complemented some of the artwork in the coffee shop, and he told me it was his work—he was a graphic design artist. I told him about Woodside. My enthusiasm inspired him to support our idea. Whenever you're trying to get anyone behind your ideas, enthusiasm is key. Why would anyone get excited about an idea if you weren't excited?

My friend quickly got to work and made fantastic T-shirt designs that fit perfectly with our company's vision. Meanwhile, I began to promote our brand with everyone I knew. Even though we didn't really have a full-scale product, I was persistent, because many people have to repeatedly hear things before it becomes part of their permanent memory. When we launched our initial line, many people where already aware of it and more susceptible to buying our brand.

A college friend, who also had a T-shirt business, once asked me, "Ivan, how is it that I see your shirts on campus, but I can't give mine away?"

I told him, "I am not selling them a shirt; I am selling them a piece of me. I focus on what I do best and not do everything such as design, make, sell, and market the shirts." I recruited those who had the resources and talent to help launch my idea.

Your book of thoughts and ideas:

This will be your tool to keep track of the way you think. Throughout your day, write down anything that sparks an idea. At the end of the day, write down what the general theme of your thoughts was for the day.

Some things to think about:

1. What music did you listen to?

2. What book did you read?

3. What did you learn today?

4. How can you implement what you learned?

In time your book can be an amazing record keeper on your mental progression. It's a great way to spark ideas that have been brewing in your consciousness from days to months. By constantly reviewing your book, your mind will construct associations and patterns from the random ideas and thoughts you wrote down, and one day you might think of a radically, new, useful idea that grew from all the randomness. Learn to observe how your friends analyze their surroundings. You might think of a brilliant idea by observing how your friends react to their surroundings. You might discover a need that is underserved.

7 DEVELOPING YOUR OWN UNIQUE STYLE

Develop your own style

You will know when you have become a person of influence, because your persona, charisma, aura will draw people to you. When I was in college, people often told me that it seemed like I knew everyone. People knew I had a lot of friends, but not once did they ask how I knew so many people, until one day one of my friends jokingly said, "Man Ivan you should write a book about how to make friends." We all laughed, but later I really considered it and analyzed why I make so many friends. Once you become aware of what it is that you exactly do, and not just a subconscious action, then you have more control over your actions. In my case, I developed my style further and became more influential.

Think of others as your inner self-reflection. If you talk about an idea with someone and you feel that they are unsure about it, that should tell you that deep down you are also possibly unsure about it. If you have people that constantly treat you in a bad way, be honest and ask yourself if that is how you feel about other people. People can be a great source of feedback of your inner self. I observed what made me be influential to a particular person, and that helped me develop my style.

Analyze how you act, talk, dress, think, etc. and if you feel that they are unique elements of your personality, use them more often, exaggerate them, make them truly yours and only yours. If you say one word in a particular way, own that word, have the mentality that this is my word and no one can say it better than me. If you have that certain swagger in your step, exaggerate it so that everyone knows that's you just by the way you walk. You become imprinted in people minds by the way you act and talk, because you do not act like everyone else. People don't mimic or imitate what they perceive to be normal and average. Once you truly become aware of what little things define you, the more you will embrace your differences and people will embrace you.

I have a lot of mannerisms when I am communicating with people and a habit of always throwing up a peace sign in photos or when I say bye; others began to mimic me. People have the unconscious ability to mimic someone in order to communicate more effectively and have a deeper level of understanding.

Becoming observant of great things

Always be aware of your surroundings, train yourself to look for greatness in everything, and ask yourself if you can incorporate that into your identity.

In order to really influence others, you need to influence their mood. Now that you know what makes you special, use all those things to boost people's moods when they are around you. After a while people make the association that whenever they see you, they will feel good.

Go Abroad

Studying or travelling abroad helps you contrast everything you have ever known and gives you a better understanding of the world. You also realize how much you are influenced by your society. When I was in Europe, I realized that I am someone who likes a slowed down pace in life. I caught myself racing around in an environment that was telling me to slow down.

I realized how fast we move in America and I didn't like it. Sometimes you have to experience an opposite scenario to gain a deeper understanding. When you only experience things in a certain way people become accustomed to it and don't question it. I loved seeing Europeans read their newspaper at a Café for three hours with no sense of being rushed.

Working and Living Abroad

www.transitionsabroad.com A great resource if you plan to work, study, or live abroad.

www.workingoverseas.com Find a job in another country.

www.meetup.com When you get to your new destination, you are going to want to make some friends as soon as possible. Use this site to find people all over the world who share the same interests as you.

www.eslcafe.com Teaching English in another country is a great way of supporting yourself and learning about the culture.

www.bridgetefl.com Helps you get your teaching credential's that are recognized internationally.

Volunteer to gain a new perspective:

Check out:

http://www.globalvolunteers.org

http://www.crossculturalsolutions.org

http://www.alternativebreaks.org

Playing Games: A great way to practice and increase creativity while having a more meaningful learning experience.

"People have enough to live, but nothing to live for; they have the means but no meaning" Robert William Fogel

8 MASTERING YOUR ENERGY, AWARENESS, INTENT AND MINDSET

Any internal chatter in your mind is a symptom of you saying no to life and the present moment. Internal chatter is the fight between the identity you show to the world and the identity that you believe is your inner world. The identity you project to the world will always be more than what you really are.

Time is circular, that's why things move from the present to the past continuously. As soon as you think you are in the present moment, you are lost because you are thinking thoughts that are already in the past.

"Events come and go. This is the wheel of Maya. Let the wheel spin around you without attachment to any part of it. Let go of the spokes. Live in the center. That is the real" - Babaji

Technique: The way to center yourself into the present moment is to always remember that you simply exist in each moment (you are not your mind), thus repeatedly bringing you back to the present. You have to be able to distinguish your true identity from your mind. Your mind is when you are thinking. When you are aware that you are thinking, that awareness is not part of thinking.

Internal Wandering

By constantly seeking and becoming aware of your inner space, you will notice that your life becomes an unpredictable adventure. You will become more acquainted with your inner silence that is always available to you, which will lead you to the insights of your life's decisions. The outside world will begin to change, because your internal dialogue has changed. By constantly seeking your inner silence you will notice that your life becomes in tune with your seeking of personal truths.

Your joy and suffering come from the perspective of self-centeredness. Expand your awareness and be aware of everything; feel the clarity that comes from understanding that the ultimate meaning you get depends on the level that it relates to your self-centeredness. The more that you are grounded in your center inner being, the more your external reality makes sense to you, and the better you respond to it. The moment that you realize your self-centered consciousness, you stop acting self-centered. Acting self-centered is wrong but being clear that you are self-centered is not wrong, by nature this is the only way you can perceive your reality.

Right action +wrong reason = wrong result

Inner awareness is critical to making appropriate decisions in your life. Without awareness, you will make decisions based on a previous experience, which may or not may be true in the present moment. For example, think of the time you had a conversation with a person and told yourself you would not forget to bring up that point next time you spoke on the same topic. Next time, you are speaking about the same topic forget to make the point, because you were operating on a lower awareness.

When you have awareness of your inner decision-making process you will never be lost. This type of awareness leads to inspired actions.

Anytime you are able to grasp or perceive something, your mind has gone to work and is now the past. If you continuously drop your last thought, and move on to the new thought, you will be in the present moment. With enough practice, you will be able to experience how things really happen in your life, not simply by an event you are trying to make sense of from memory. As soon as you finish a thought, it will involve thinking to drop it. The best technique is to live the process in itself and it will grow within you. Live your life by each second—learning to leave and not hold onto anything, you will live your life in the present moment. Simply learn to observe things with no judgment and attachment; this will happen when you no longer interpret your environment for ego purposes.

By living and acting from the present moment, you will be continually growing and evolving your identity, because every day you are updating your inner ideas about who you are. If you go to bed and realize that when you wake up in the morning, you are not the same person who went to bed last night, you will be on the right track to expand your awareness and consciousness.

Make it a habit to monitor your mental and emotional state through self-observation.

Good questions to ask yourself are:

--"Am I at ease at this moment?"

--"What am I feeling inside me at this moment?"

By becoming more conscious and observant of how you feel on the inside, you will be better able to handle your external reality. Your emotions are simply reactions to your thoughts

If you are constantly thinking in terms of being somewhere else and not being content with where you presently are, you are denying the experience of the present moment.

In order to change that you have three choices:

--Remove yourself from the situation

--Change the situation

--Or totally accept it

Keep in mind that when you choose to take some type of action, it comes from a place of personal insight rather than from a place of negativity.

Increasing your awareness

The best way is to begin paying attention to the vibration and sensation of your body.

Example: When you look at something, pay attention to how you feel and become aware of it.

Exercise: When I was living in Prague, one of my favorite things to do was to walk to a park, pick a bench, close my eyes, and try to tune into every sound around me. The more you practice at directing your attention, the more you become aware of everything you experience.

Observe the observer (your inner witness). Once you make this realization you will be able to add intention to your thoughts. You will also begin to develop a memory of your observer, so that as everyday events happen you will have insight into everyday coincidences.

Creating Your Reality

Throughout your day, you need to be conscious and aware of your thoughts, when you pause and contemplate, because they are in the space of where they will be sent to your subconscious mind. Our conscious mind cannot help but analyze and judge all of our thoughts. Depending on the sum of all your knowledge and your beliefs, those thoughts will be modified and eventually sent and carried to your subconscious mind. These thoughts, whether they are true or not, will influence your attitude and how you respond to the outside world, ultimately creating your reality. Your subconscious mind does not think it simply receives and sends data without any judgment.

Your Common Thought

When you are unaware of your common thought, you are completely unaware of your enemy within. Reality reflects back to you what you think commonly. Many people are not aware of their common thought because they think that that is who they are. You are not your mind and thoughts, only a certain aspect of you. You have been conditioned to associate your thoughts with your identity and sense of self. To see who you really are is to transcend this association and observe your mind and thinking processes.

Thinking without awareness is how many people become slaves to their mind. Their mind takes on its own imagination leading you helplessly in infinite directions. Therefore, your identity also follows because you are only experiencing the world by believing that who you are is your thoughts and mind. Each day you have thousands of thoughts and you become emotionally consumed by them. The only way you will ever be at peace is to disassociate your self-image and identity from them. This requires a shift in your consciousness that will allow you to be the witness and observer of your thoughts and ego. This is the consciousness and perspective of the real you. The more this becomes a habit, the more you will become liberated from incessant thinking.

This shift will allow you to see how you lived your life before you made this distinction. It can be very subtle, but now you are able to see what direction in life you want to take. You simply are not just moving because your mind is telling you too. You will find yourself being attached to the thoughts and things that you feel define you as a person. Your ultimate realization will be when you know and feel that your true identity is consciousness itself, rather than what your consciousness had identified with.

You need to discipline yourself to think only in terms of the unlimited and expanded. Speak only in reference to that mind state, until this becomes your common thought. When you pause and contemplate throughout your day, it is being done from a beneficial common thought. Your words are very powerful, because they are the ending to a thought process. When you say, "I am so stupid," even if you don't mean it, you are programming your neural networks.

Don't integrate time into your visualizations of the things you want to create in your life. Any time you add time to your thoughts, you have already analyzed your thoughts and set up backup thinking processes to provide a way out. For example, if you visualize and focus on your vacation to Hawaii, you begin to analyze and tell yourself that if you can't make it happen in six months, you will make it happen within a year. Your final thought is impregnated in your subconscious mind and but instead of doing it in six months, you will do it in 12 months, if it even happens. When you were thinking of doing in it in six months you had some doubts come into play. This is why you need laser beam focus—being absolutely clear in what you want and how you think, in order to create the reality the way you really want it.

There will be times when you will be put in extremely uncomfortable and painful situations and will begin to think that it's impossible to not entertain those negative thoughts. Your will power is what you are going to need to overcome those situations.

To give you an idea of how powerful your subconscious mind can be, think about people who have been hypnotized. These people have simply been put into a mind sate where the suggestions are being sent to their unconscious mind unfiltered. They are in a state of mind of no thinking, simply sending and receiving. People who never knew they had certain talents perform what they have been asked to do without hesitation. Condition yourself to be unconditional and that whatever you focus on should be unconditional and timeless.

How to see the world through other people's eyes

Another great thing to do to increase your awareness is to continually practice seeing the world and yourself through the eyes of others.

Exercise: When you wake in the morning, practice staring at yourself in the mirror and visualize that you are in the mirror looking at yourself from that perspective. This practice will help you with accepting yourself and others.

You will also learn to see things from other people's perspectives and points of view.

When looking at the mirror, really concentrate on feeling that you are in the mirror, until you feel a click or shift that you are looking back at yourself. When you are in a public place, practice on achieving that feeling and perspective by transferring your awareness to another person's eyes. The more you practice this, the more you feel like you know what a person is thinking and feeling.

** **Special Bonus:** I have added one of my most popular blog post that gives a good overview of increasing your self-awareness.

How To Increase Your Awareness and Expand Your Consciousness

"The only thing that interferes with my learning is my education." Albert Einstein

Awakening Consciousness

When I take a look at our society as a whole and think about the stage of evolution that we are at, it amazes me how many problems still exist on earth. We have advanced tremendously in technology and commerce, but one thing we have neglected to advance is the world's consciousness, the ability to be awake in the world.

Any problems we have come from a lack of awareness. If our politicians where really conscious there would be no question about right and wrong, they would be able to make the right decision. In pure awareness there is no dark only light. In fact, if everyone was really awake and conscious, the role of government would be very limited, because people would not depend on someone else to lead them.

We live in the age of information, but even with all the knowledge of the world at our fingertips, what good does it really do us if we are not conscious and awake?

The problem is that knowledge essentially binds us, the more knowledge a person gains, the more asleep that he becomes. The more knowledge he gains the more entrenched his mind becomes in a certain way of thinking. He may think he is thinking outside of the box, it's the same box; he just makes it look different.

"When I examine myself and my methods of thought, I come to the conclusion that the gift of fantasy has meant more to me than my talent for absorbing positive knowledge."- Albert Einstein

Just really take a good look at the world around you; you will realize that most of the population is operating from a level where they are asleep. Today's society has become extremely efficient at doing things with little to no awareness, we just run on auto pilot. Once you realize how much you really are operating on auto pilot in your day-to-day life, you will be able to search for ways to become more aware.

Think about the very first time you were learning to drive, remember how engaged you where? You could feel every movement you made, you were fully present in what you were doing, you were in a state of heightened awareness. After a few weeks all your motions where effortless, you could look at your rear-view mirror, adjust your stereo, and change gears with very little awareness.

Levels of Consciousness

Your mind has different levels of consciousness. First is your conscious mind, and then behind your conscious mind is the subconscious mind. If you learn to pay close attention you can hear the subconsciousness' whispers. Then behind the subconscious mind is the unconscious. The unconscious is who you really are, behind your thinking mind, behind your body, the essence of your very nature. Behind the unconscious is what Dr. Jung called the collective unconscious, which is the whole of humanity's evolution until now.

In order to become more conscious and aware and rise above the unconscious state, you need to experience being alert and awake. This is something you cannot just simply understand logically or philosophically, because it will only remain as an intellectual understanding.

"The intuitive mind is a sacred gift and the rational mind is a faithful servant. We have created a society that honors the servant and has forgotten the gift." - Albert Einstein

It is going to take a real effort to wake yourself up, to discover your true potential, to become aware that you are far more than what you appear to be.

How Do You Start Becoming More Aware?

You have to learn to become observant and watchful. Learn to observe and be a witness to every act you do, every thought that passes your mind. Watch every desire that bubbles up within you. Observe even seemingly little things like your gestures, walking, talking, breathing, eating; everything can be an opportunity to watch.

You will realize that the more watchful that you become, that your internal chatter will become less and less. Your thoughts become more manageable and you gain a new clarity. A clear mind is a happy mind. As you grow in your awareness, your inner growth will explode because you begin to let the deepest parts of your being rise to the surface.

You will also come to notice how much of your growth was being suppressed by the awareness of the whole (society) and dependent on others. At this lower level of awareness, you observe how people mostly try and grow by means of arguing, simply trying to outwit, and outsmart others on pure logic.

One day while drinking some coffee I observed two people arguing, the person who feels that he came out on top is puffed up in his ego, and all he did was make a brilliant logical explanation to satisfy his own desires. The other person now feels bitter towards the other, did not accept the other person's point of view, and still chooses to keep his own beliefs.

I can see that both are oblivious to what actually happened. Nothing was accomplished, but in their minds, they felt something was achieved. They were simply not aware of what was going on inside themselves; being lost on the inside is being lost on the outside.

Awareness Steps to Achieve Spiritual Growth

Step 1: The Body – learn to become aware of your body first. Learn to place your attention and sense your body's energy from the inside out. Learn to feel its presence, its aliveness. You can begin by starting in small parts of the body, such as your hands, until your attention can encompass your whole body.

Step 2: Your Thoughts - Once you become observant of your body, expand your awareness to observe and watch your thoughts.

Step 3: Feelings and Emotions – When you are able to watch your thoughts learn to watch your feelings and emotions.

When you are watchful of your body, thoughts, feelings, and emotions your awareness will begin to operate from a state of inner harmony.

Step 4: Aware of your own awareness - When you live a life of inner harmony, that harmony allows you to be in a position to become of aware of your own awareness.

When you are able to be aware of your own awareness you will realize how cunning the mind is, and how great it is at rationalizing. Rationalizing is not awareness; awareness means that whatsoever is happening in the moment is happening with complete consciousness, that you are fully present.

The problem lies in that all the mind can do is think of the past and imagine the future. To be present and totally aware is to be in the space of no thought, dropping your analogical mind. Also try and understand that dropping the mind does not mean to be in a vegetative state, it is simply a space where you move into a deeper depth of understanding and perspective.

Your mind is only able to work linearly, from point A to point B, from one thought to the next. If you move vertically that is a movement of consciousness, which is awareness.

Learn to continually bring yourself to the present. When you catch yourself living in the past or imagining the future, bring your awareness back to the present moment. Do not feel bad when you realize you are not in the present; this is just a habit you need to gradually get out of until your new habit is being more in the present.

One important thing to remember also is to not make the mistake of constantly thinking "how can I be in the present moment", because this involves thinking; this is a very delicate line.

Just learn to be a passive witness, which means you observe without judgment, and slowly you will fall into moments of beautiful silence. By constantly being in a state witnessing you will fall into the gaps between your thoughts.

"The important thing is not to stop questioning. Curiosity has its own reason for existing. One cannot help but be in awe when he contemplates the mysteries of eternity, of life, of the marvelous structure of reality. It is enough if one tries merely to comprehend a little of this mystery every day. Never lose a holy curiosity." – Albert Einstein

Awareness is Key to Spiritual Transformation

With whatever you find yourself doing, learn to continuously be aware of whatever is going on inside you. The more you become aware of yourself doing whatever it is that you are doing, the more you become centered in your inner being.

Once you begin to be stronger inside, you will develop a deeper feeling of the inner presence that you "are". Your energies will become concentrated around this centered presence, and your true self is born. Ego is only a false sense of self, but if you don't awaken your inner self you will go on believing that you have a self that is only your ego.

When you have little or no awareness of your inner world, you are a victim of circumstances because you operate only by reaction. From this level your physical senses rule, your physical senses only job is to respond. You only take action when something has been done to you.

When you are grounded in your inner being you create a distance between your inner being and your physical senses. Something can affect your physical sense but cannot touch your inner self. When you take actions from the center, your actions are total and complete, inspired actions not hindered by past and future.

You will come to find that becoming a witness of your life will be something that should be done passively. Learn to do what you are doing non-verbally; verbalization is escaping from the experience.

When you look at the Stars in the sky with awe and admiration you feel a deep connection of beauty within you. As soon as you try to verbalize what you are feeling, you remove yourself from it, because to verbalize is to think, and to think is to not be fully present.

Learning to be non-verbal in your internal world will make you the witness of your inner world. Language is only needed to communicate with others, but language is not needed to communicate with oneself.

Thoughts come and go, think of your mind as the host and your thoughts as the guests. Once you learn to watch, witness, and observe your thoughts, you will be in a position of mastering your mind.

Your thoughts are there but you are no longer a slave to your thoughts, you are the master of your thoughts. Don't try and control your mind, this is impossible, just learn to become centered in your consciousness. Just watch, don't try and stop your mind, just observe it and allow it to happen on its own.

Being aware and clear headed will allow you to take responsible actions, because any action you take born out of awareness is total and complete. Any action you take will be action that arises from your watching.

With Awareness You Can Be Decisive

Only awareness can be decisive because your mind only conceives possibilities and is constantly in a state of indecisiveness.

Many people strive to be a man or woman of character, but a man or woman of character only reacts. Character is mechanical because it operates from memory; moral conditioning on what is right and wrong.

The problem with this is that life is constantly changing, it is never the same. But a man of character always responds with the same answers. A man of consciousness simply takes action, and whatever action he takes in the moment is natural and perfect for the situation.

Becoming a man of awareness will also allow you in seeing your own faults. The moment you become aware of your faults they will begin to disappear. They were only allowed to exist because you where unconscious of it.

So, don't be worried about errors and mistakes in your life. Put all your energy and effort into becoming a more conscious awake being. In a state of pure awareness your faults can't exist. Someone who tries to be a good person requires great effort. A conscious person needs no effort, living a conscious life makes you a good person.

Someone trying to be good is constantly judging himself and others, his inner world is one of continuous conflict. He condemns and represses and learns to hide it in the deepest parts of his being.

You are good by just being aware. There is no question of whether what you do is good or bad, from awareness whatever you do is good. A person of awareness is calm, relaxed, quiet, serene, creative, only good can come from these states of being.

You will know when you become a person of awareness because you will quit watching others, that's what everybody else does; all you need to do is watch yourself.

9 CONCLUSION

I want to sincerely thank you for making it to the end. I tried to make this guide as simple as possible while trying to provide the most practical value for you. This is by no means a definitive guide. It was just my sincere hope that this short eBook interests you to walk a path of personal discovery, giving you a better sense of how you can accomplish anything by constantly working on your own blueprint.

Maybe now you will be able to see what pieces of the puzzle you were missing or want to improve upon. If you had never been interested in meditation, I hope that I piqued enough interest in you to learn about the teachings of the great Yogi Masters of India, who developed the tools for self-realization for thousands of years. If you never saw yourself as a marketer, I hope I gave you enough insight that you can really spread and get your message across with enough effort. If you have never seen yourself as an influential person, maybe we will meet one day, and you can give me some new pointers. I truly believe we are all incredible beings with unlimited potential to create and change the world in a positive way. Do not wait. Waiting is a waste of time. Show this world what you're made of and go GET YOUR SHINE ON! I am counting on you!

To read my latest articles go to freedomfromtheknown.com and follow me on Twitter, let's change the world together!

If you enjoyed this book, please consider leaving your review and any feedback you may have. I really appreciate your support!

"The only goal worth attaining is complete freedom to be yourself, without illusions and false beliefs" - Deepak Chopra

10 BONUS RESOURCES:

Your Online Traffic Blueprint: Use this as a guide to show you all the different mediums you can use to spread your message and how they relate and affect each other.

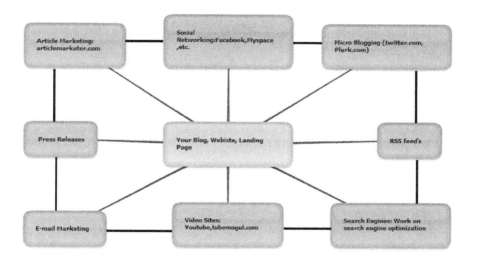

Traveling Resources:

www.virtualtourist.com: Travel Guides, Maps, Forums, Deals....

www.escapeartist.com

www.gridskipper.com: Gridskipper is the decadent guide to the best in worldwide urban travel—hotels, restaurants, clubs, flights, and sights.

www.lonelyplanet.com

www.worldtravelwatch.com: Stay informed of world events and odd happenings before you take flight on your adventure.

www.irs.gov: Make sure you keep Uncle Sam happy while you are traveling or living abroad.

Cheap Air Fair:

www.orbitz.com

www.priceline.com

www.easyjet.com

www.skyeurope.com

www.1800flyeurope.com

www.skyscanner.net

Free Worldwide Housing:

www.couchsurfing.com: While I lived in Prague, I had many friends who let travelers on a budget crash on their couches. It was a great way to meet new and interesting people, making worldwide connections.

www.globalfreeloaders.com: This is an online community, bringing people together to offer you free accommodation around the world. Save money and make new friends while seeing the world from a local's perspective!

www.hospitalityclub.org

Cheap Accommodation:

www.hostels.com

www.hostelworld.com

Communications:

www.skype.com: Stay in touch with your friends and family with this free Internet Phone.

www.freetranslation.com

ABOUT THE AUTHOR

To learn more about me, check out my website at:
freedomfromtheknown.com

Where I write about my experiences in:
- self-development, psychology, and mysticism
- traveling and living abroad
- meditation, yoga, lucid dreaming
- entrepreneurship
- language learning
- how to live in the now

Printed in Great Britain
by Amazon

78720646R00068